WORLD ...

VIDÁLIA
SWEET ONION

COOKBOOK
AND
ONIONS NATIONWIDE

World Famous Vidalia Sweet Onion Cookbook

Re-order
Additional Copies
from

Vidalia Cookbooks
Rt. 1 Hwy 56 East
Uvalda, GA 30473

We Ship
Vidalia Sweet
Onions
Nationwide

In May and June <u>only</u> of each year, we ship Vidalia Onions Nationwide. We ship in sizes of Jumbo, Medium and Pee Wees, in 50-lb., 25-lb. and 10-lb. bags. Please call or write us in March, April, May or June and we can furnish you prices, shipping and handling charges for this season. Remember we only ship in May and June.

Morris Farms
Rt. 1 Hwy. 56 East
Uvalda, GA 30473
912-594-6533

Austin
Randall
Howard

A Gourmet's Delight

Introduction
to
Vidalia Sweet Onions

Vidalia Onions were first grown in the Vidalia area in the early 1940's. It soon became known that these onions were extremely mild. In years to come as customers would place their orders for onions, they would become known as Vidalia Sweet Onions. In the 40's and 50's and 60's the onion acreage was still very small. In 1974 there were still less than 200 total in acres of Vidalia Onions grown. From 1974 on, the demand for Vidalia Onions grew very fast, and so did acreage produced. In 1989 there were approximately 6,000 acres of Vidalia Onions planted. Vidalia Sweet Onions are grown from the F-I Hybrid Yellow Granex onion seed. Other varieties of onion seed have been planted, but so far the F-I Hybrid Yellow Granex is the most popular seed by far.

We are asked the question almost every day, "Why are our onions <u>sweet</u> or <u>extremely mild?</u>" We think it is our soil conditions, but we really don't know. Vidalia Sweet Onions are planted basically the same as all onions are planted nationwide, although it is very expensive from seed planting to harvest time to produce an acre of Vidalia Gourmets. The seeds are planted in September. The plants are planted in November and December to be harvested the following year in May and June. The months of planting and harvesting may vary some due to weather conditions. Vidalia Onions demand tender, loving care through many months of Mother Nature's best to produce our World Famous Vidalia Sweet Onions.

CONTENTS

Continued

•

Printed in the USA by

WIMMER
The Wimmer Companies, Inc.
Memphis • Dallas

So what better time than now to include onions on the menu? Nothing can even come close to an onion in versatility. It can make an appearance in the soup, salad, and the main course, improving the flavor of all of them, without seeming repetitious.

Whether they are baked, boiled, fried, stuffed, sauteed, glazed, creamed, steamed, barbecued or raw, they are an easy way to make meals different and exciting.

Storing and Caring for Onions

Onions should be stored in a well ventilated, dry place. Don't store them in piles; single layers ensure longer life. Old panty hose are an excellent place to keep them. Just slide an onion in and tie a knot. Slide another in and tie a knot etc. An extra refrigerator which is still running is another excellent place to store dry onions. Chopped fresh onions will stay fresh in a screw top jar in the refrigerator for several days.

To remove onion pungency from the hands, rub well with vinegar, salt or lemon juice. Then wash hands in hot water and soap.

- *All Natural, No Preservatives*
- *Made from Juicy Sweet Vidalia Onions prepared and handpacked in Uvalda, Georgia*
- *Great for Gifts and Special Occasions*

Vidalia Onion Relish
a traditional favorite of Vidalia fans.

Vidalia Onion Relish With Mustard
We've added mustard for a spicy taste treat!

Barbecue Sauce
Have a backyard barbecue with a Vidalia flair!

Pickles
A great way to enjoy the famous Vidalia taste all year long!

Vinaigrette
Turn your salad into a Vidalia delight, without any oil!

To find out more about these delicious items, call or write:

Morris Farms
Route 1, Highway 56 East
Uvalda, Georgia 30473

1-800-447-9338

All these items can be shipped to your door.

Vidalia Onion Delights

Vidalia Onion Sandwich

Stop laughing now, take hold of yourself. You won't believe it until you try it.

Spread mayonnaise as desired on two slices of sand-wich bread of your choice. Take one thick juicy slice of Vidalia Sweet Onion and salt and pepper lightly. Combine this and you have Vidalia's Finest.

Vidalia Onion Cookies

½ cup margarine
1 cup sugar
1 cup chopped cooked Vidalia onions
1 cup cooked squash
2 cups flour
1 teaspoon baking powder
1 teaspoon baking soda
½ teaspoon salt
1 tablespoon cinnamon
1 teaspoon vanilla

Cook onions in small amount of water until tender. Cream together margarine, sugar, onions and squash. Sift together flour, baking powder, baking soda, salt and cinnamon; add to creamed mixture. Add vanilla; beat well. Drop from teaspoon on a greased cookie sheet. Bake at 375 degrees for 12-15 minutes.

Yield: 5 dozen cookies.

Pee Wees the Greatest

This is my favorite. Peel small pee wee onions and dip into onion ring batter. Fry until a golden brown. This is simply delicious; you must try it!

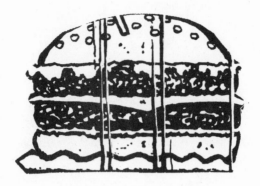

Don't Forget
America's Favorites

1. A big, thick, juicy hamburger with lettuce, tomato and a thick slice of Vidalia Sweet Onion.

2. Crispy fried chicken, fresh creamed corn, fresh butter beans, fried okra, hot homemade corn bread with butter (wow), iced tea and a thick, juicy slice of Vidalia Sweet Onion.

3. Always top off your favorite hot dog with chopped Vidalia Sweet Onions.

4. An old fashioned fish fry is never complete without sliced Vidalia Sweet Onions.

Notes - Recipes

Notes - Recipes

Appetizers, Soups, Breads & Sauces

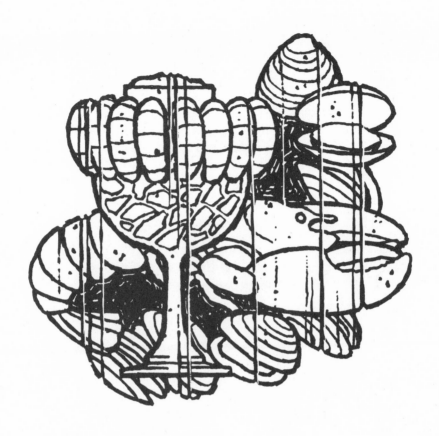

Shrimp Balls with Vidalia Onions

    1 medium Vidalia Onion
    1 medium raw potato
    1 ½ pounds raw shrimp
    1 egg
    salt & pepper to taste
    oil for frying

    Grind onions, potatoes, and shrimp. Stir in egg, salt and pepper. Batter must be thick. Drop by teaspoons into hot oil and fry until brown.

Shrimp Spread

1 (8 oz.) package cream cheese
½ cup mayonnaise
1 (4½ oz.) can tiny shrimp (drained)
½ cup finely chopped celery
½ cup finely chopped onions
1½ teaspoon lemon juice
1½ tablespoon worcestershire sauce

Combine softened cream cheese and mayonnaise; beat until smooth. Blend in remaining ingredients. Mix well, chill and serve with crackers. Yields 2 cups. Best when refrigerated overnight.

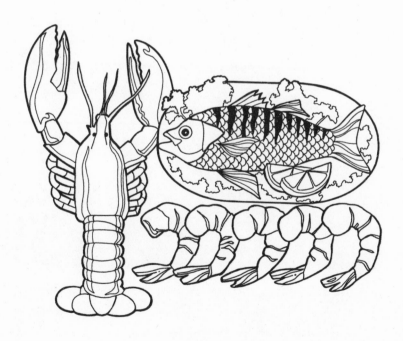

Vidalia Onion Dip

1 jumbo or 2 medium Vidalia Onions, chopped
3 tablespoons sliced black olives
3 tablespoons olive oil
1 ½ teaspoons wine vinegar
dash of worcestershire sauce
3 tablespoons chopped green chili peppers
1 large or 2 medium tomatoes, peeled and chopped
dash of tobasco sauce
salt and pepper to taste

Combine the above ingredients and chill well. Serve
with corn chips.

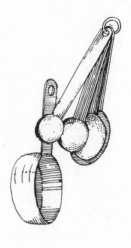

Hamburger ⁃ Vidalia Onion Soup

1 tablespoon butter
½ pound hamburger
12 medium Vidalia Onions, thinly sliced
1 can beef stock
1 cup water
2 beef bouillon cubes

Brown butter, add hamburger; fry until brown and well separated. Add onions, beef stock, water and bouillon cubes. Simmer for 30 minutes. Serve with buttered toast and Parmesan cheese.

Chuck's Italian Onion Soup

4 medium Vidalia Onions
4 (4 inch square) slices mozzarella cheese
1 (½ oz.) can Parmesan cheese (shredded)
1 cup Italian bread crumbs
2 (8 oz.) cans beef broth
½ stick butter (not margarine)
4 oven tempered soup bowls

1. Chop onion to chewable size.
2. Take 4 slices of bread and cut into small crouton size then bake until golden.
3. Preheat oven at 350 degrees
4. Saute onions in butter on low heat till soft and dark brown. Salt and pepper to your own taste.
5. Take both cans of beef broth plus 1 cup water and cook to slight boil, adding bread crumbs, onions and sauce.
6. Take and pour all broth with onions into each soup bowl immediately. Then add parmesan cheese and croutons to each bowl equally, then layer each bowl with slice of mozzarella cheese. Place into oven. Bake till cheese is crisp and brown. Let sit for a few minutes, then PRESTO! its-a Italian!!

Onion Cheese Soup

2 cups chopped Vidalia Onions
3 tablespoons flour
½ teaspoon salt
dash of pepper
4 cups milk
2 cups sharp American cheese

Cook chopped onions in butter until tender, but not brown. Blend flour, salt and pepper. Add milk all at once. Heat and stir until boiling. Remove from heat. Add shredded cheese, stirring to melt cheese.

Serves 4 to 6.

Potato and Vidalia Onion Soup

¼ cup butter
2 large Vidalia Onions, sliced
2 medium potatoes sliced
2 quarts water
1 tablespoon salt
¼ cup butter
½ cup cream
3 tablespoons chives

Saute onions in butter until wilted.   Add potatoes,
water and salt; bring to boil.   Simmer 45 minutes.   Remove from heat.

Blend cooked mixture until smooth.   Return to saucepan, add butter, cream and chives.   Check for seasoning.
Heat (do not boil or cream will curdle).

Vidalia Onion Flatbread

Chewy rounds of skillet-cooked bread with sauteed onions mixed into the dough are good as a snack or as a savory accompaniment for soup, salad, or cheese.

Makes about 28 rounds.

½ cup lightly salted butter
4 cups diced Vidalia Onions (about 1 ¼ pounds)
3 ½ cups unbleached all-purpose flour
2 ¾ teaspoons salt
1 to 1 ¼ cups cold water
¼ pound slab bacon or bacon drippings

Heat butter in medium skillet over high heat until hot; reduce heat to medium high. Add onions; saute, stirring occasionally, until soft but not brown, 5 to 10 minutes. Cool.

Mix 3 cups of the flour and the salt in large bowl. Add 1 cup of the water, the onions and their liquid; stir to form a soft dough (use part or all of the remaining ¼ cup water if needed). Knead dough on lightly floured surface to form smooth dough, using as much of the remaining flour as needed to prevent sticking.

Tear off small pieces of dough, slightly larger than an unshelled walnut. Roll on floured surface into 4-inch rounds.

Heat large heavy skillet over medium high heat; rub with bacon to coat lightly with fat. Place as many rounds of bread in skillet as will fit in single layer; cook until lightly browned on bottom, 5 to 8 minutes. (if breads begin to get too dark, reduce heat.) Turn rounds and brown the second side, about 8 minutes. Remove breads; keep warm wrapped in cloth. Repeat, rubbing skillet with bacon as needed and cooking remaining pieces of dough. Serve flatbread warm.

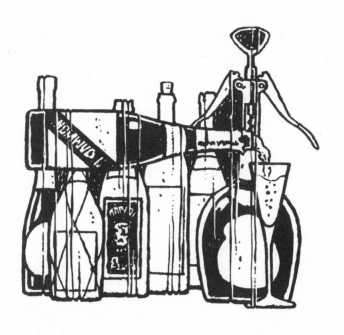

Vidalia Onion-Cheese Bread

½ cup chopped Vidalia Onion
Butter
1 beaten egg
½ cup milk
1½ cup biscuit mix
1 cup grated sharp cheese
2 tablespoons minced parsley

Saute onion in small amount of butter until tender but not brown. Combine egg and milk; stir into biscuit mix only until mix is moistened. Add onion, ½ of the cheese and parsley; mix well. Spread in greased 8 x 1½-inch pan. Sprinkle with remaining ½ cup cheese; drizzle 2 tablespoons melted butter over top. Bake in preheated 350 degree oven until bread tests done.

Vidalia Onion Supper Bread

½ cup chopped Vidalia Onions
2 tablespoons butter or margarine
1 package corn-muffin or corn-bread mix
½ cup dairy sour cream
½ cup shredded sharp process American cheese

Cook onion in butter till tender but not brown. Prepare mix according to package directions. Pour into greased 8 x 8 x 2 inch pan. Sprinkle with cooked onion. Mix sour cream and cheese; spoon over the top. Bake in hot oven (400 degrees) 25 minutes or till done. Let stand a few minutes; cut in 9 squares.

Vidalia Onion Sauce

4 ounces sliced Vidalia Onions
¾ cups water
¾ cups skim milk
1 envelope instant chicken broth and seasoning mix
salt

Cook sliced onions in saucepan with water, milk and broth mix until onions are soft and water and milk cooks down to half. Puree in blender or put through strainer; season with salt. Use with fish, veal, lamb, sweetbreads or hamburgers.

Makes four servings.

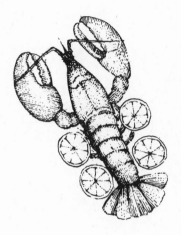

Vidalia Onion Mayonnaise

Puree 2 medium Vidalia Onions with a little water in a blender, then mix with 1 cup mayonnaise until smooth. Flavor with dash of cognac.

Vidalia Onion Bits
Bar-B-Q Sauce

1 gallon white vinegar
1 gallon ketchup
juice of 1 large fresh lemon
1 ea. Jumbo Vidalia Onion chopped fine
¼ cup pure prepared mustard
¼ cup worcestershire sauce
1 teaspoon salt
3 teaspoons onion salt
1 teaspoon garlic salt
2 teaspoon liquid smoke
1 teaspoon paprika
2 cups sugar
3 teaspoons black pepper
2 teaspoons hot sauce
4 teaspoons soy sauce
½ stick butter

Combine all ingredients and bring to a rolling boil. Stirring almost constantly, let boil for ten to fifteen minutes then simmer for about two hours. Simply delicious on all meats.

Granny Price's Fish Sauce

¼ cup worcestershire sauce
2 tablespoons vinegar
¼ cup sugar
1 cup ketchup
1 cup grated Vidalia Sweet Onions

Cook 5 minutes on slow heat on top of stove to serve over fish or any seafood.

Notes - Recipes

Notes - Recipes

Salads & Pickling

Vidalia Onion Salad

3 cups thinly sliced Vidalia Onions
1 large head lettuce, torn in bite size pieces
8 hardboiled eggs, sliced

Dressing:
½ cup mustard
½ cup mayonnaise
Onion salt to taste
1/8 lemon and pepper seasoning salt
2 teaspoons white vinegar

Mix all ingredients together. Make layers of salad by starting with ½ of lettuce, ½ of onion, ½ of eggs. Pour ½ of dressing over the combination. Repeat layers, using remaining sauce on top. Cover and chill for two hours. Very good with steak and potatoes.

Stuffed Vidalia Onion Salad

5 to 6 large Vidalia Onions
1 (8 oz.) cream cheese
2 tablespoons deviled ham
1 teaspoon salt
dash pepper

Peel onions. Remove centers of onions. Whip cream cheese until soft and creamy. Blend in deviled ham and remaining ingredients. Fill centers with mixture and chill until firm. To serve, slice onions and serve on lettuce leaves.

Serves 6 to 8.

Cucumbers and Vidalia Onions

2 cucumbers
1 large Vidalia Onion
½ cup dark vinegar
½ cup water
pepper to taste
¼ teaspoon salt
¼ cup sugar

Slice cucumbers and onion. Place in a bowl. Sprinkle a little salt over them and set aside.

Combine the remaining ingredients in a saucepan. Heat until hot not boiling. Pour over cucumbers and onions. Let cool, then cover and refrigerate.

Note: It tastes better the second or third day as the flavor blends. Keep refrigerated.

Layered Salad

1 head of lettuce, broken in large bowl
1 large Vidalia Onion, chopped fine
5 ribs celery, chopped fine
1 16 oz. can small English peas (drained)
1 large bell pepper, chopped fine

Spread and seal with 1 cup of mayonnaise. Then top in this order:

2 tablespoons sugar
1 cup Parmesan cheese
5 slices bacon, crisp, crumbled

Seal with aluminum foil, refrigerate overnight or 12 hours. Serve as is--do not stir. This will last for a couple of days if kept refrigerated.

German Potato Salad

Boil about a dozen medium size potatoes <u>unpeeled.</u> (Peel after they are cooked.) Slice into bowl.

Cut 4 strips of bacon into pieces, fry slowly till brown. Cut a Vidalia Onion into small pieces and cook in bacon fat, until golden. Add the following ingredients and cook until thick. Pour over potatoes.

Dressing:

5 tablespoon sugar

¼ cup vinegar

¾ cup water

1 tablespoon salt

1 tablespoon (heaping) cornstarch

2 tablespoon bacon fat

¼ teaspoon dry mustard

Serves approximately 8 people.

Kiwi - Vidalia Onion Chutney

2 cups cider vinegar
1 1-pound box brown sugar
1½ teaspoon salt
1 teaspoon ground ginger
¼ teaspoon cayenne pepper
2 cups pared diced apples
1 cup thinly sliced onions
1 cup raisins
½ lemon, thinly sliced
3 cups chopped kiwi fruit

Combine first 5 ingredients in large saucepan; cook over low heat until reduced to about half. Add apples, onions, raisins, and lemon; cook for about 10 minutes. Add Kiwi fruit; bring just to boiling point. Chill well. Serve with poultry, pork or ham. May be blended in a blender and poured over block of cream cheese to spread on crackers as appetizer.

Vidalia Onion Relish

3½ pints chopped onions
½ pint chopped cabbage
½ pint chopped bell pepper
½ cup pickling salt
6 cups boiling water
¼ cup dry mustard
¼ cup flour
1 cup sugar
½ tablespoon turmeric
1 tablespoon celery seed
½ tablespoon white mustard seed
1 pint white vinegar

Combine vegetables and salt, cover with boiling water. Let stand overnight. Squeeze dry by twisting nylon net to remove moisture. Make dressing of remaining ingredients, heat to boil, stirring constantly until thickened. Add vegetables and cook until thick, again stirring constantly to prevent scorching. Seal in hot sterile jars. Let stand for two to three weeks.

Pickled Vidalia Onions

(about 7 pints)

4 quarts tiny onions, peeled
1 cup salt
2 cups sugar
¼ cup mustard seed
2½ tablespoons prepared horseradish
2 quarts distilled white vinegar
7 small hot red peppers
7 bay leaves

To peel onions, cover with boiling water; let stand 2 minutes. Drain; dip in cold water; peel. Sprinkle onions with salt; add cold water to cover. Let stand 12 to 18 hours in a cool place. Drain, rinse and drain thoroughly. Combine sugar, mustard seed, horseradish and vinegar; simmer 15 minutes. Pack onions into jars, leaving ½ inch head space. Add 1 hot pepper and 1 bay leaf to each jar. Heat pickling liquid to a boil. Pour, boiling hot, over onions, leaving ½ inch head space. Remove air bubbles. Adjust lids. Process 10 minutes in boiling water bath.

Spiced Green Tomato Pickles
(5 pints)

4 quarts green tomatoes (about 24 to 28 medium)
2 cups onions (about 6 to 8 medium)
½ cup salt
2 green bell peppers, finely chopped
3 cups white or brown sugar
1 quart distilled white vinegar (approximately)
2½ tablespoons celery seed
2½ tablespoons mustard seed

Tie in a spice bag:
2 tablespoons whole cloves
2 tablespoons whole allspice
3 sticks cinnamon (3-inch pieces)

Wash and drain vegetables. Cut tomatoes into slices or quarters; peel and slice onions. Sprinkle alternative layers of tomatoes and onions with salt. Cover and let stand overnight in a crock or enamel vessel. In the morning drain thoroughly. Transfer to a pan and add peppers, sugar, loose spices and spice bag. Add enough vinegar to cover the mixture. Bring to a boil and simmer 15 minutes, or until vegetables are tender. Remove spice bag. Pack vegetables into jars, leaving ½ inch head space. Fill jar to within ½ inch of top with boiling hot liquid. Remove air bubbles. Adjust lids. Process 15 minutes in a boiling water bath.

Notes - Recipes

Notes - Recipes

Casseroles, Vegetables & Meats

Vidalia Onion Casserole

6-7 large Vidalia Onions
1 stick margarine
Parmesan cheese
Ritz crackers

Peel and slice onions into thin rings. Saute in margarine until done. Pour half of onions into 1½ quart casserole, cover with Parmesan cheese then crushed Ritz crackers. Repeat layers and bake uncovered in 325 degree oven until golden brown, about 30 minutes.
Yield: 7 servings.

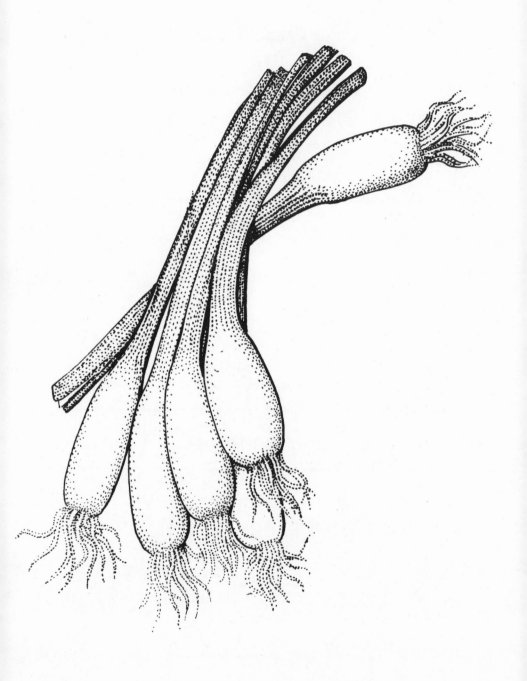

Vidalia Sweet Onion Grits

8 slices bacon
1 (16 oz.) can tomatoes, undrained and chopped
1 medium Vidalia Onion, chopped
2 small green peppers, finely chopped
¼ teaspoon sugar
6 cups water
1 teaspoon salt
1½ cups uncooked regular grits

Cook bacon slices in skillet until crisp. Drain bacon; crumble and set aside. Pour off drippings, reserving two tablespoons in skillet.

Saute onion and green pepper in drippings; stir in tomatoes and sugar. Bring to a boil; reduce heat and simmer 30 minutes, stirring occasionally.

Bring water and salt to a boil; add grits. Cook 10-20 minutes, stirring frequently, until grits are thickened. Remove from heat; stir in tomato mixture. Spoon into serving dish; sprinkle bacon on top.

Yield: 8 servings.

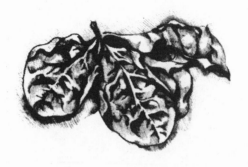

Spinach-Stuffed Vidalia Onions

4-5 medium Vidalia Onions
1 pound fresh spinach, stems removed.
2 tablespoons melted butter
¼ cup Half and Half
salt and pepper to taste
grated Parmesan cheese

Peel onions; core out hole in center. Put in water and steam. Do not overcook until soft and mushy. Remove from heat and cool.

Wash spinach and cook one minute, using only the water that clings to the leaves, drain and chop.

Saute spinach in butter. Add Half and Half and cook until fairly dry. Season with salt and pepper. Fill onions with spinach mixture; sprinkle with cheese. Bake in a greased shallow pan at 350 degrees until onions are thoroughly heated.

Barbecued Beans

4 slices bacon, cubed
1 onion diced
½ cup catsup
1 teaspoon mustard
2 tablespoons vinegar
4 tablespoons brown sugar
1 teaspoon salt
1 can kidney beans
1 can pork and beans
1 can limas
1 can green beans

Brown bacon and onion in skillet. Drain juice from lima and green beans. Combine all ingredients and heat.

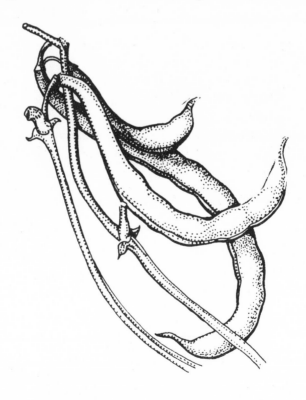

Peas Supreme

1 cup ham, cooked and diced
1 can English peas, drained
1 cup grated mild American cheese
1 can cream of chicken soup
¼ cup diced Vidalia Onions
¼ cup pimento, chopped and drained
1 cup rice, cooked

Mix all ingredients and bake in a greased casserole dish at 325 degrees F. for 30 minutes. (Optional: may top with French fried onion rings or buttered bread crumbs.)

Vidalia Onion Quiche

1 pie crust, unbaked, pricked
¾ cup Vidalia Onions
½ cup ham diced
3 tablespoons margarine
1½ cups mild American cheese, grated
1 cup Swiss cheese grated
1 cup caraway seed cheese, grated
¼ cup evaporated milk
3 eggs
½ cup Sour Cream
½ cup crumbled bacon

Melt margarine in skillet and saute onions and ham until done. Place in bottom of unbaked pie crust. Mix cheese, milk, eggs and sour cream and pour atop onion and ham mixture. Bake at 350 degrees F. for 30 minutes and garnish with crumbled bacon. Can be served for a brunch with fresh fruit.

Ham and Broccoli Quiche

2 frozen pie crusts
1 cup cooked chopped ham
2 eggs, beaten
¾ cup grated cheddar cheese
¾ cup grated or thin slices Swiss cheese
1 (10 oz.) package frozen chopped Broccoli
chopped Vidalia Onion to taste
1 small can or jar chopped mushrooms, drained
⅓ cup of milk
salt and pepper

Cook broccoli according to directions, drain and pour in bowl. Add 2 beaten eggs, all of the cheeses, mushrooms, onions, milk, salt, pepper and chopped ham.

Pour into both pie crusts. Bake at 375 degrees for about 50 minutes.

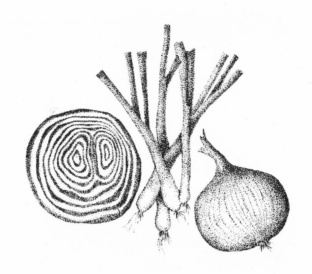

Vidalia Onion Pie

2 pounds thinly sliced Vidalia Onions
1 stick butter
3 eggs, beaten
1 cup sour cream
¼ teaspoon salt
½ teaspoon pepper
dash tabasco
1 pie shell unbaked
grated Parmesan cheese

Saute onions in butter. Combine eggs and sour cream. Add to onion mixture. Season and pour in pie shell. Sprinkle with cheese. Bake at 450 degree for 20 minutes, then 325 degrees for 20 minutes.

Serves 6

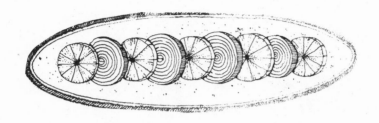

Vidalia Onion Pie

1 cup Ritz cracker crumbs
½ stick butter, melted
2 cups Vidalia Onions, thinly sliced
2 tablespoons butter
2 eggs
¾ cup milk
¾ teaspoon salt
dash pepper
¼ cup grated sharp cheddar cheese
paprika
parsley

Mix Ritz cracker crumbs and melted butter. Press into 8 inch pie plate. Saute onions with 2 tablespoons butter until clear, not brown. Spoon into pie crust. Beat eggs with milk, salt pepper and pour over onions. Sprinkle with cheese and paprika. Bake at 350 degrees for 30 minutes or until center is firm. Sprinkle with parsley before serving.

Vidalia Onion Pie

1 baked pie shell
3½ cups thinly sliced Vidalia Onions
3 tablespoons melted butter
½ cup milk
1½ cups sour cream
1 teaspoon salt
3 tablespoon flour
2 eggs (well beaten)
Bacon slices

Saute onions in butter until lightly browned. Spoon into pie shell. Add milk and 1¼ cup sour cream. Stir flour with ¼ cup sour cream. Combine with egg mixture; pour over onion mixture. Bake at 325 degrees F. for 30 minutes or until firm in center. Garnish with crisp bacon. (Use parsley flakes as optional garnish.)

Chow Chow

(about 8 pints)

10 large onions, peeled and chopped
6 green bell peppers, seeded and chopped
6 red bell peppers, seeded and chopped
2 heads cabbage, chopped
4 hot red peppers, seeded and chopped
12½ pounds green tomatoes, cored and chopped
4 firm apples or pears, cored and chopped (optional)
2 cups sugar
1 quart vinegar

Tie in a spice bag:
2 tablespoons mustard seed
2 tablespoons celery seed
4 sticks cinnamon (3-inch pieces)
2 tablespoons whole cloves

Sprinkle the onions, peppers, cabbage and tomatoes
with 3 tablespoons salt. Let stand 4 hours; drain. Mix
vinegar and sugar; add spice bag. Bring to boil, stirring
constantly. Add chopped vegetables and boil 10 minutes.
Remove spice bag. Pack hot relish into jars, leaving
½ inch head space. Adjust lids. Process 15 minutes in
a boiling water bath.

Spicy Meatballs in Sweet-Sour Sauce

1½ pounds ground beef round
½ pound ground lean pork
1 cup milk
½ cup fresh whole-wheat bread crumbs
1½ teaspoons salt
½ teaspoon ginger
½ teaspoon allspice
¼ teaspoon freshly ground white pepper
1 cup sweet onions, minced
1 tablespoon unsalted butter

Mix beef and pork. Put through meat grinder 3 times until texture is very fine or process, half at a time, in food processor fitted with steel blade, until meat is smooth, 15 to 30 seconds.

Combine meat, milk, bread crumbs, salt, ginger, allspice and pepper in large bowl. Let stand 5 minutes.

Heat oven to 500 degrees F. Saute onions in butter in small skillet until soft, about 2 minutes. Add to meat mixture; mix thoroughly. Shape mixture into very small balls, about 1 rounded teaspoonful each. Place in jelly-roll pan. Bake until lightly browned, 10-15 minutes. Transfer to clean baking pan; cool. Freeze in pan in single layer. Transfer to airtight containers. Freeze up to 1 month.

Makes 80.

continued on next page

Reheat in Sweet-sour Pineapple Sauce.

Sauce:
2 cans (15½ ounces each) pineapple chunks in
  natural juice
¼ cup cornstarch
¼ cup (packed) brown sugar
1 cup chicken stock or broth
¾ cup white wine vinegar
1 tablespoon dark soy sauce
1 tablespoon ketchup
1 cup Vidalia Onions
1 large green bell pepper, seeded and cut into
  ½ inch squares
1 can (8 oz.) water chestnuts, drained

Just before serving time, drain pineapple, reserving
1¼ cups of the juice. Mix cornstarch and brown sugar
in large saucepan; stir in reserved pineapple juice, the
stock, vinegar, soy sauce and ketchup. Heat over high
heat, stirring constantly, to boiling. Reduce heat to
medium-low. Cook, stirring constantly, until sauce
thickens and bubbles for 2 minutes. Add onions and
green pepper; cook and stir 1 minute.

Gently stir frozen meatballs, pineapple chunks and
water chestnuts into sauce; reduce heat to low. Cook,
covered, until meatballs are heated through, about 15
minutes. Keep warm in a chafing dish or warming tray.

Sausage Stuffed Vidalia Onions

¾ pound bulk mild pork sausage
½ teaspoon thyme
½ teaspoon sage
1 teaspoon chives
1 cup Vidalia Onions, chopped
¾ cup mushrooms, sliced
2 cups cheddar cheese, grated
1 cup sour cream
4 Vidalia Jumbo Onions, split and cored

Split and core 4 Vidalia Onions. Arrange in a greased casserole dish. Cook sausage, spices, onions and mushrooms until brown. Drain off excess grease and add cheese and sour cream. Mix well. Stuff Vidalia Jumbo Onions with mixture. Bake uncovered 350 degrees F. for 45 minutes or until desired doneness. Serve hot.

Delicious with soup and can be served as the main entree.

Steak Slices with Vidalia Onions

1 pound top round or sirloin beef
1 tablespoon dry sherry
1 tablespoon cornstarch
1 tablespoon soy sauce
1 medium Vidalia onion
¼ cup vegetable oil
pepper as desired

Cut beef into chunks that will fit chute. Place in freezer until firm, but not completely frozen. Lock bowl into position and insert Slicer Disc. Place cover in position. Using pusher press meat against blade and process to slice. Combine sherry, cornstarch and soy sauce in bowl. Add meat slices. Toss and allow to marinate 15 to 20 minutes. Slice onion using Slicer Disc. Pour oil into large skillet. Heat oven medium high (375 degrees F. electric skillet). Add meat slices and onion. Stir fry until cooked to desired doneness.
Makes 4 servings.

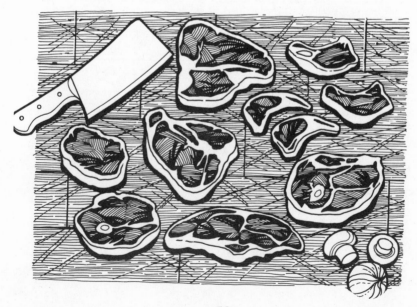

Vidalia Onions with Liver

1 ½ pounds calves or baby beef liver cut in
  1 inch strips
½ teaspoon salt
1/8 teaspoon pepper
¼ cup butter or bacon drippings
2 Vidalia Onions, thinly sliced
1 (8 oz.) can sliced mushrooms, undrained
2 cups dairy sour cream
1 teaspoon worcestershire sauce

1. Season liver with salt and pepper. Preheat skillet to 325 degrees. Melt butter and saute onions until tender. Add liver and brown on all sides.

2. Add mushrooms with liquid; reduce heat to simmer. Simmer covered with vent closed for 8-10 minutes.

3. Add sour cream and continue cooking for an additional 8-10 minutes. Add worcestershire sauce. Makes 6 servings.

Vidalia Onion Canape

6 large onions
½ pound hot sausage
Pepperidge Farm Dressing Mix
Bouillon
Salt to taste
Cayenne pepper to taste

Boil onions until soft; drain and cool. Cook sausage until crumbly and brown. Add enough dressing mix and bouillon to make a thick stuffing. Season to taste with salt and cayenne. Separate onions into large leaves. Place a generous amount of dressing on each leaf and roll up like an old fashioned cigarette. Refrigerate until ready to serve. Brown under broiler before serving.

Sausage-Stuffed Mushrooms

2 dozen large fresh mushrooms
1 package (12 ounces) sausage meat
1 small green pepper
1 small Vidalia Onion
1 teaspoon oregano
½ cup sour cream
Salt and pepper to taste

Wash mushrooms, wipe dry and remove stems. Chop mushroom stems, onions and green pepper until fine. In a large skillet, crumble the sausage meat and cook over medium heat until brown. Drain off fat, add onion, green pepper and mushroom stems. Cook, stirring occasionally until onion is limp. Add spices and stir in the sour cream. Don't allow mixture to boil.

Place mushroom caps in a shallow casserole. Place a spoonful of sausage mixture in each cap. You may cover the mixture with plastic wrap and refrigerate. Shortly before serving, broil until the caps are tender and sausage mixture is hot, 5-10 minutes.

Seven Layer Casserole

In 2 quart baking dish layer the following:

    1 cup uncooked rice, washed and drained
    1 cup canned whole kernel corn
    Sprinkle with salt and pepper
    Pour over 1 can tomato sauce and ½ can water
    ½ cup each Vidalia Onion and green pepper
    ¾ to 1 pound ground beef uncooked
    Salt and pepper
    Pour over a second can of tomato sauce &
        ¼ can water
    Cover with 4 strips of bacon

Cover; bake 1 hour, uncover and bake about 30 minutes at 350 Degrees.

Poor Boy's

1 pound hamburger
1 large Vidalia Onion
1 or 2 potatoes

Fix hamburger in patties (thick). Slice onion and potatoes. Wrap one hamburger, one slice onion and one slice potato in a square piece of tin foil. Fix as many of these you like and place in oven and bake at 350 degrees until done. Serve on buns with mayonnaise or mustard.

Wild Rice Casserole

1 box wild rice
1 medium Vidalia Onion, chopped
1 (3 oz.) can sliced mushrooms
½ bell pepper, chopped
½ pound sausage
Dash tabasco
1 teaspoon Accent
salt and pepper
1 can cream of mushroom soup

Prepare rice as instructed on box. Brown sausage in skillet, then saute onions and green pepper. Add crumbled sausage and vegetables to cooked, drained rice. Stir in seasonings and mushroom soup and bake uncovered in a casserole dish for 25 to 30 minutes, at 350 degrees F.

Vidalia Onion Shells

5 jumbo Vidalia Onions
1½ pounds ground beef
1 small can chopped mushrooms, undrained
1 large green pepper
1 tablespoon salt
1 tablespoon soy sauce
1 tablespoon Worcestershire sauce
2 tablespoons butter or margarine

After peeling outer skin of onions, slice onions in half horizontally. Remove onion centers leaving 2 thick outer rings for shells. Chop onion centers up real fine, then chop green pepper. Brown ground beef in butter or margarine, then drain. Mix together in large mixing bowl, drained ground beef, salt, onions, mushrooms and pepper. Add soy sauce and worcestershire sauce. Knead all ingredients thoroughly, then stuff into onion shells. Place in shallow baking dish with cover. Bake at 300 degrees or 350 degrees approximately 30 minutes. Upon removal from oven, liberally douse the center of each onion with red hot sauce to add color and flavor.

Makes 10 shells (5 servings).

Turkey Creole

2 cups turkey broth
2 ½ cups (No. 2 can) tomatoes
¼ cup chopped green pepper
½ cup chopped Vidalia Onion
½ cup chopped celery
2 cups diced cooked turkey
1 teaspoon salt
1 teaspoon sugar
1 small tip bay leaf
⅔ cup uncooked rice

Brown chopped onion, chopped green pepper in small amount of fat. Add chopped turkey and uncooked rice. Add remaining ingredients, cover and simmer until tender and rice is done.

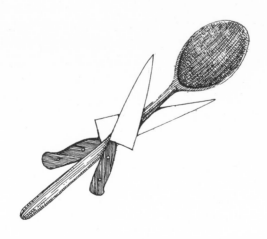

Chicken Casserole

4 cups chicken, diced, cooked and deboned
1 can cream of chicken soup
1 cup Vidalia Onions, chopped
½ cup bell pepper, chopped
¼ cup pimento, diced
1½ cup rice, cooked
½ stick margarine, melted
½ cup mayonnaise
1 teaspoon salt
½ teaspoon black pepper
1 small can water chestnuts, sliced and drained
1 small can mushrooms, sliced and drained

Crust:
2 cups crushed saltine cracker crumbs
¼ cup margarine, melted

Mix all ingredients except crust and placed in a greased casserole dish. Bake at 350 degrees F. for 30-35 minutes. Take from oven and top with cracker crumbs and margarine. Return to oven and bake until brown (3-5 minutes).

Chicken Breasts and Ham with Fast Cooking Wild Rice

3 small chicken breasts, cut in half
2 tablespoons butter or margarine
¼ pound mushrooms, sliced
½ cup finely diced cooked ham
3 green onions, sliced
2 teaspoons flour
½ teaspoon salt
1/8 teaspoon leaf thyme
⅓ cup dry white wine (optional)
1 pkg. (6¼ oz.) long grain and wild rice
1 medium tomato, chopped

Brown chicken breasts on both sides in butter or margarine in 10 inch skillet. Remove chicken from skillet. Add mushrooms, ham and green onions; cook until mushrooms are heated. Stir in flour, salt and thyme. Add wine. Return chicken breasts to skillet, skin side down. Cover and cook over low heat until chicken is tender, 25 to 30 minutes. Turn skin side up after 15 minutes. Cook rice according to package directions. Stir tomato into hot cooked rice.

Makes 6 servings.

Vidalia Onion-Stuffed Chicken

Before placing the whole chicken on the spit for roasting, place a peeled whole Vidalia Onion inside for flavor.

VIDALIA
SWEET
ONIONS
Morris Farms
Uvalda, GA

Baked Vidalia Onions

Peel number of large Vidalia Onions desired. Core the centers ¾ way down. Place 1 tablespoon butter in each and sprinkle with salt and pepper. Affix one or two strips of bacon to top of onion with toothpicks. Wrap tightly in foil and bake for 30 minutes or until tender at 350 degrees.

Baked Vidalia Onions

Vidalia Onion
Butter
salt and pepper
Worcestershire sauce

Peel onions. Core out center ¾ way down. Place on
a sheet of tin foil. Sprinkle with salt and pepper. Stuff
with butter and 1 teaspoon worcestershire sauce.
Wrap lightly and bake at 350 degrees for approximately
45 minutes or until tender.

Baked Vidalia Onions

Peel the onion, core out center ¾ way down, then salt and pepper. Stuff with butter, then wrap in tin foil and bake at 350 degrees until tender.

Jim's Baked Vidalia Onions

Peel a large Vidalia Onion and core out center of onion ¾ way down. Salt and pepper lightly. Pack ⅓ butter, ⅓ bacon bits and ⅓ Monterey Jack cheese. On outside of onion wrap with 2 strips of bacon and secure with toothpick. Wrap onion in tin foil being careful not to puncture foil. Pre-heat oven to 350 degrees and bake approximately 40-45 minutes. Check occasionally as you would for baked potato for desired softness.

Vidalia Onions Baked on Coals

Wrap large, peeled Vidalia Onions in aluminum foil as you do with baked potatoes and bury them in the hot ashes to come out and go with your baked potato and steak.

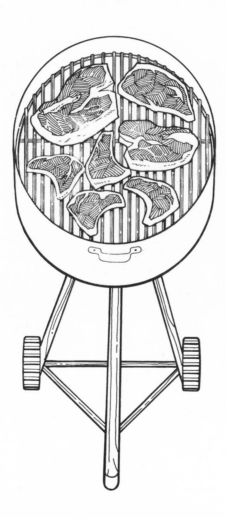

Baked Vidalia Onions

1. Preheat oven to 375 degrees
2. Wash 1 Vidalia Onion for each person to be served
3. Place unpeeled onions in a shallow baking dish.
   Bake for 1-1½ hours, until onions are tender.
4. When tender, cut a slice from each onion and slip
   the skins off.

Serve hot with butter, salt and pepper or cold with
lemon juice.

Stuffed Vidalia Onion

1 large Vidalia Onion per serving
1 tablespoon butter per serving
1 box stove top dressing, mixed according to
  package directions but not cooked

Peel and core onions, stuff centers with dressing and top with butter. Wrap each onion separately in foil. Bake at 350 degrees for 45 minutes.

Sweet and Sour Vidalia Onions

5 large Vidalia Onions
¼ cup cider vinegar
½ cup melted butter
½ cup boiling water
½ cup brown sugar

Slice onions and arrange in 1 quart baking dish. Mix rest of ingredients and pour over onions. Bake at 300 degrees for one hour.

Almond-Stuffed Vidalia Onions

6 medium Vidalia Onions, about 3 inches
  in diameter
¼ teaspoon sage
1/8 teaspoon thyme
¾ cup coarsely chopped almonds
¼ cup margarine, melted
1½ cups croutons
1 cup apple juice
¾ teaspoon salt
¼ teaspoon pepper

Cut a thin slice off root end of each onion; cut a
¼-inch slice off opposite end. Carefully remove center
of each onion with vegetable parer or melon ball cutter,
leaving a 3/8-inch shell (at least 2 rings). Arrange onion
shells in ungreased 2-quart casserole.

Toss almonds, croutons, salt, pepper, sage thyme and
butter. Fill each onion shell with stuffing. Spoon any
remaining stuffing on top of onions. Pour apple juice
around onions.

Bake covered 40 minutes at 325 degrees F. Uncover
and bake until tender, about 20 minutes.

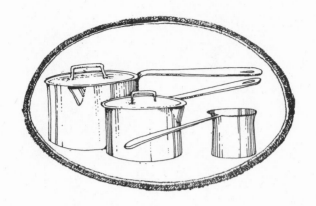

Vidalia Onions in Madeira Cream

4 large Vidalia Onions, thickly sliced
8 tablespoons butter
½ cup Madeira Wine
salt and freshly ground black pepper
¼ cup heavy cream
¼ cup finely chopped fresh parsley

Melt butter in a wide, heavy pan. Add the onion slices and turn them in butter to coat them thoroughly. Cover the pan and cook over very low heat for 10 minutes, shaking the pan occasionally.

Uncover the pan, increase the heat slightly and stir in the Madeira. Cook stirring frequently, until the Madeira evaporates and onions are soft and lightly caramelized.

Season to taste with salt, and pepper and stir in the cream and parsley. Bring to a boil then reduce the heat and simmer for 1 minute,

Serve hot. The onions are marvelous with steak, liver or any grilled meat.

Creamed Vidalia Onions

3 cups sliced Vidalia Onions
¼ cup butter, melted
2 tablespoons all-purpose flour
1 teaspoon salt
¼ teaspoon dried thyme, crushed
1 cup milk

Cook onion, covered in a large amount of boiling salted water till tender, 20-25 minutes. Drain. In saucepan mix butter, flour, salt, thyme and dash pepper. Blend in milk; cook, stirring constantly, till thickened and bubbly. Stir in onions slices. Heat through.
Makes 6 to 8 servings.

Crusty Eggs with
Vidalia Onion-Celery Sauce

Yield: 8 servings

    8 hard-cooked eggs
    2 pounds bulk sausage meat
    1 cup grated Vidalia Onion
    1 cup fresh breadcrumbs
    2 eggs, well beaten
    1½ cups finely crushed cornflake crumbs

Sauce:
    ¼ cup butter
    1 cup chopped Vidalia Onion
    1 cup chopped celery and leaves
    ¼ cup flour
    2 cups milk
    2 envelopes dehydrated chicken broth or
      3 bouillon cubes
    Salt and pepper
    Celery leaves

Shell hard-cooked eggs. Place in cold water to cool completely. In a bowl mix sausage meat, grated onion (drain off any liquid), fresh breadcrumbs, and half of beaten eggs. Remove eggs from cold water. Dry completely so sausage meat coatings will adhere. Divide sausage mixture evenly into eight parts and use to encase each hard-cooked egg. Coat sausage meat with beaten eggs and then roll in cornflake crumbs. Chill at least 30 minutes. Bake coated eggs in preheated 350 degree F. oven on a shallow greased baking pan for 35 - 40 minutes, or until deep brown and crusty.

Meanwhile, prepare sauce. In a medium saucepan, melt butter. Saute onions, celery and leaves until tender, about 5 minutes. Stir in flour, cook 30 seconds. Slowly blend in milk. Cook over low heat, stirring constantly until sauce bubbles and thickens. Stir in dehydrated chicken broth, salt and pepper to taste. Serve sauce over eggs.

Barbecued Vidalia Onions

5-6 large Vidalia Onions
¼ cup French salad dressing
1 teaspoon worcestershire sauce
1 (8 oz. can) tomato sauce
¼ teaspoon chili powder
dash cayenne pepper
Parsley for garnish

Cook onions in water with salt until almost tender. Drain and place in buttered baking dish. Mix remaining ingredients except parsley. Pour over onions. Bake at 400 degrees for about 45 minutes, basting several times. Test with fork for tenderness. Serve sprinkled with fresh parsley.

Scalloped Vidalia Onions

5-6 large Vidalia Onions
1 stick butter
2 tablespoons flour
1 teaspoon salt
½ teaspoon pepper
1 teaspoon dry mustard
1 cup milk
8 ounces cheese
Crumbs from Pepperidge Farms Herb Stuffing
Butter for topping

Thinly slice onions to equal about 4 cups. Saute in ½ stick of butter. In saucepan melt remaining ½ stick of butter and stir in flour and seasoning. Slowly stir in milk and grated cheese, cook slowly until cheese is melted. In a 1 quart baking dish alternate layers of onions and sauce. Sprinkle top with crumbs and dot with butter. Bake at 400 degrees for 20 minutes.

Serves 6.

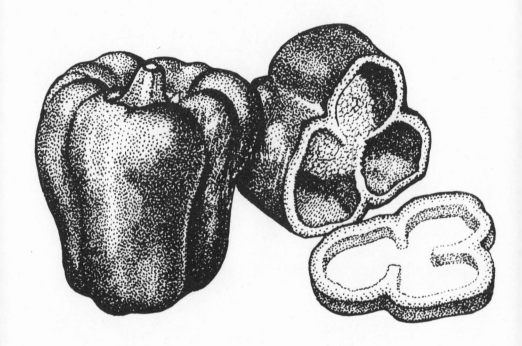

Sauteed Green Peppers

10 medium size green peppers
4 medium size Vidalia Onions
1 cup sliced celery
4 tablespoons melted butter or margarine
½ cup parlsey
¼ cup beef broth
1 teaspoon salt
¼ teaspoon pepper

Remove seeds from green peppers and cut peppers into rings. Saute green peppers, onion, celery and parsley in butter. Cover and cook for 5 minutes. Add remaining ingredients; cover and simmer about 20-25 minutes or until tender.

Baked Yellow Squash

2 pounds yellow squash
1 chopped green pepper
1 chopped Vidalia Onions
2 grated carrots
Small package of Pepperidge Farm Herbed
  Seasoned Stuffing mix.
1 can cream of chicken soup
½ pint Sour Cream
1 stick butter

Cook squash until slightly tender in small amount of water. Melt butter and mix with Herb Seasoning. Combine ¾ of mix with all other ingredients and sprinkle rest of mix on top. Bake in a 350 degree oven for 30 minutes.

Squash Casserole

2 cups squash, cooked and drained
1 medium Vidalia Onion, chopped
½ stick margarine, melted
1 can cream of chicken soup, undiluted
4 ounces sour cream
1 egg
2 cups cheese, grated
1 large can French fried onion rings

Mix first seven ingredients together and place in greased casserole dish. Bake at 350 degrees F. for 30-35 minutes or until done. Remove from oven and top with French fried onion rings. Brown and serve while hot.

Stuffed Onion Potatoes

4 large baking potatoes
2 large onions
1 cup chopped green onions
½ cup chopped mushrooms
½ cup cheddar cheese, shredded
¼ stick melted butter

1. Core out potatoes leaving skin unharmed.
2. Take inner potatoes and chop for boiling, then boil potatoes till soft and ready for whipping.
3. While waiting for potatoes to boil, bake skins till crisp, trying not to harm the skins. (300 degrees.)
4. Whip potatoes as you would mashed potatoes. mix onions and mushrooms into whipped potatoes, adding melted butter and salt and pepper as desired.
5. Then stuff baked potato skins with your whipped potatoes and bake for 20 minutes at 350 degrees. 5 minutes before removing from oven, sprinkle cheese and green onion on top.

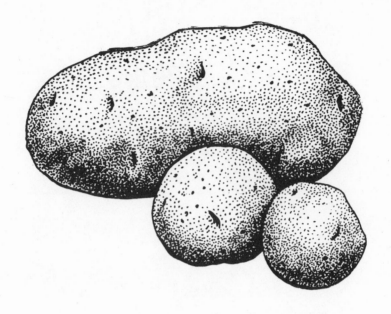

Vidalia Onion
and Potato Casserole

6-7 large Vidalia Onions
6-7 large white potatoes
2 cans condensed mushroom soup
2 pounds lean ground beef
salt
pepper

Season meat and brown in skillet. Peel and slice potatoes and onions thinly. Alternate layers of potatoes, onions, and meat. Pour mushroom soup over all and bake at 350 degrees for 45-55 minutes.

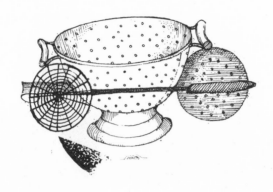

Scalloped Potatoes

3 tablespoons margarine
2 tablespoons all purpose flour
3 cups milk
1 teaspoon salt
½ teaspoon pepper
1-2 large Vidalia Onions
6 medium potatoes, peeled and sliced

Make sauce of first ingredients (except onions and potatoes). Place half the potatoes in greased 2 quart casserole. Cover with half the onions and half the sauce. Repeat layers cover and bake at 350 degrees about about one hour. Before serving, you may sprinkle grated cheese over top of casserole.

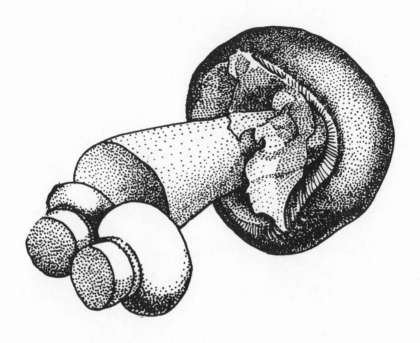

Baked Vidalia Onions
in Sherry Cream Sauce

3 cups pre-cooked Vidalia Onions
1 cup light cream
2 tablespoons pimento
½ teaspoon salt
⅓ cup sharp chedder cheese
1/8 teaspoon pepper
1 small jar sliced mushrooms
⅓ cup sherry
3 tablespoons butter

Drain onions and arrange in shallow baking dish.
Combine sherry, cream, salt, pepper, pimento and
mushrooms. Pour over onions, dot with butter.
Sprinkle with a grated cheese. Cover and bake at 350
degrees for 20 minutes.

Grilled Squash and Vidalia Onions

6-7 medium-size yellow squash, cut into ½ inch
  slices
3-4 medium Vidalia Onions, cut into ½ inch slices
¼ teaspoon garlic salt
2 tablespoons butter
salt and pepper to taste

Alternate squash and onion slices in rows on large
sheet of foil. Sprinkle with garlic salt, salt, pepper and
dot with butter. Wrap foil securely to seal. Place on
grill over moderate heat for about 45 minutes or until
tender.
    Yield: 5-6 servings.

Corn and Vidalia Onion Casserole

  1 can cream style corn
  ½ cup green peppers, chopped
  ¾ cup onions, diced
  2 tablespoons margarine
  3 tablespoons pimento, diced and drained
  4 eggs, slightly beaten

Saute green peppers and onions in margarine. Add corn, pimento and eggs. Pour in greased pan and bake at 350 degrees F. for 25 minutes or until firm. (OP-tional: may top with French fried onion rings or cracker crumbs.)

Mixed Vegetable Casserole

1 can mixed vegetables, drained
½ cup Vidalia Onion, diced
1 can cream of mushroom soup
2 cups bacon, fried and crumbled
1 teaspoon black pepper

Crust:
2 cups craker crumbs (saltines)
1/8 cup margarine

Mix all ingredients together and bake in greased casserole dish at 350 degrees F. for 25-30 minutes. Top with cracker crumbs and margarine and brown.

Vidalia Onion Ring Casserole
(Outdoor grill)

1 pound Vidalia Onions
salt and pepper
⅓ cup water
2 tablespoons butter or margarine
½ cup milk
1 egg, well beaten
½ cup grated sharp cheddar cheese
Paprika

Preheat grill.

Peel and slice onions ¾ inch thick; separate into rings. Place onion rings in 9 inch foil pan; season to taste with salt and pepper. Add water; cover onions with foil. Cook on grill until onions are tender. Uncover and dot with butter. Combine milk and eggs and pour over onions. Top with cheese and sprinkle with paprika. Cover with foil, cook on low setting for 10 minutes. To cook in oven, cook in a covered casserole dish at 350 degrees for 1 hour.

Makes 4 servings.

2 - 2 - 2

2 pounds stew meat cut in small pieces.
2 large Vidalia onions, chopped
2 cans cream of mushroom soup

Mix all ingredients. Place in covered casserole dish.
Bake at 300 degrees for 3 or 4 hours. Serve over rice
or noodles.

Cindy's Fried Onion Rings

5 large Vidalia Onions
1 ¼ cup all purpose flour
dash of salt
1 slightly beaten egg
1 ¼ cup milk
1 teaspoon vegetable oil

Combine ingredients and beat until you have a good moist batter. Slice onions about ¼ inch thick. Separate into rings and dip into batter. Drop into 375 degree F. cooking oil or shortening. When rings are a golden brown drain on a paper towel.

Vidalia Fried Onion Rings

1 ½ cups all-purpose flour
1 ½ cups beer (active or flat; cool or room
  temperature)
1 teaspoon salt
3-4 large Vidalia Onions
3-4 cups shortening or vegetable oil

Mix flour, beer and salt in bowl. Cover and allow batter to sit at room temperature for 3-4 hours. Peel onions and cut into ¼ inch slices. At end of 3 hours dip onions into batter. Fry in hot grease. Drain on papertowel. Sprinkle with salt.

Vidalia Onion Patties

Slice onion ¼ inch thick and put in cold water.

Make batter: mix well 1 egg and ½ cup milk.

Drop onions in batter then <u>cover</u> onion with pan-cake mix.

Pan fry in Wesson oil ¼ inch deep

When onions turn golden, turn over once.

When you eat them, you will sing praises for Vidalia Onions.

Rosemary-Glazed Vidalia Onions

3 pounds small Vidalia Onions, peeled
salt to taste

Glaze:
¼ cup butter or margarine
⅓ cup sugar
2 teaspoons lemon juice
½ teaspoon dried rosemary leaves.

In 3 quart saucepan add 1 inch of water to onions and bring to boil. Reduce heat and simmer covered, 20 minutes or until tender; drain water; keep hot.

Meanwhile, make glaze. In skillet, combine butter, sugar, lemon juice, and rosemary. With wooden spoon, stir over medium heat until sugar dissolves and mixture comes to boil.

Add onions. Cook, uncovered 10 minutes turning onions several times until glazed.

Makes 10-12 servings.

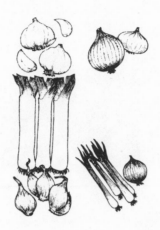

Scrambled Eggs and
Green Onion Tops

Chop up green Vidalia Onion tops and mix with your scrambled eggs. Try it, you'll find this is a pleasant change from the plain old everyday scrambled eggs.

Vidalia Cookbooks
Rt. 1 Hwy. 56 East
Uvalda, GA 30473

Please send me _____ copies of the World Famous **Vidalia Onion Cookbook**
@ $12.95 each plus $2.00 postage and handling. Each book comes packaged in a
most unique burlap bag. Georgia residents, please add 5% sales tax.

Name_____

Address_____

City_____ State_____ Zip_____

Vidalia Cookbooks
Rt. 1 Hwy. 56 East
Uvalda, GA 30473

Please send me _____ copies of the World Famous **Vidalia Onion Cookbook**
@ $12.95 each plus $2.00 postage and handling. Each book comes packaged in a
most unique burlap bag. Georgia residents, please add 5% sales tax.

Name_____

Address_____

City_____ State_____ Zip_____

Vidalia Cookbooks
Rt. 1 Hwy. 56 East
Uvalda, GA 30473

Please send me _____ copies of the World Famous **Vidalia Onion Cookbook**
@ $12.95 each plus $2.00 postage and handling. Each book comes packaged in a
most unique burlap bag. Georgia residents, please add 5% sales tax.

Name_____

Address_____

City_____ State_____ Zip_____

Reorder Additional Copies

Notes - Recipes